NO KIDDING!

INTERESTING FACTS ABOUT APRIL FOOL'S DAY

Holiday Book for Kids
Children's Holiday Books

BABY PROFESSOR

EDUCATION KIDS

Surprise! April Fool! In this book, let's find out what April Fools Day is all about.

april fool's day!

APRIL FOOLS DAY

In North America and Europe on April 1, and on some other days in different countries, the world is full of "April fools". That's the term for the tricks people play on each other on that day, and also the term for the people who get fooled. When I fool you with an April-fools prank, you are my April Fool.

But when did this strange event develop? And what do people do? Let's find out!

april
fool!

WHEN DID IT START?

We don't really know when April Fools started. Possibly the oldest tradition like April Fools is from Iran. The thirteenth day of the Persian New Year is a day for outdoor parties, including games and pranks. The tradition goes back over two thousand years. At the end of the day, you throw away some green vegetables, hoping to throw away with them any bad luck you might have for the new year.

APRIL
1

In England, Geoffrey Chaucer wrote The Canterbury Tales before 1392. In one of the tales a fox plays a trick on a proud rooster. Chaucer doesn't use the term "April Fools", but the story takes place, in most versions, "Since March began thirty days and two...", which would be March 32, or April 1. Chaucer is probably describing an existing tradition, not making up a new one.

In France in 1508, a poet refers to "poisson d'avril": "the April fish", the term for April Fools in French. Even today in France, on April 1 people often try to secretly tape paper fishes to the backs of other people's shirts, to mark them as April fools.

In 1698 in England, some people got special invitations to go to the Tower of London for the "ritual of the washing of the lions" On April 1. No such event was planned. Much later, in 1857, people lined up for tickets for the April 1 washing of the lion statues in Trafalgar Square—another event that did not exist, and that was a continuation of the joke from 1698.

PRANKS PEOPLE PLAY

People sometimes spend a lot of time setting up April Fools pranks, but some of the most effective ones take very little effort. You could set all the clocks in the house ahead or behind one hour (although this doesn't work so well nowadays, when people have cell phones to check). If you have a sister or brother, you could carefully turn your his or her shirts inside out and then hang them back up or fold them carefully and put them back in the drawer. You could switch what's in the salt cellar and the sugar bowl...but be ready to clean up when somebody spits out his breakfast cereal!

HERE ARE SOME GREAT
PRANKS PEOPLE HAVE PLAYED:

E mily and Nancy were twins in the same school, in different classes. One April 1, Emily's teacher accused her of being Nancy and trying to fool him, marched her off to Nancy's class and forced her to change places with the real Nancy. Both girls spent a very confused half hour in classes they were not prepared for, before they figured out they were April Fools.

In Scotland and Ireland, a traditional prank went like this: I give you an important letter to hand-deliver to another person. That person opens the letter and sees this verse: "Do not gawk, do not smile. Send the fool another mile." That person is supposed to write the same verse in a new letter, address it to another person, tell you that that person has the answer you need, and send you on your way. The game is to see how many people you visit before you realize you are the April Fool.

In one company where the boss liked to rush into his office at the last minute before the morning conference call, the staff filled up his office with helium balloons so he could not reach his desk.

The actor who played the Genie in the musical Aladdin went to the wax museum one April 1 and replaced the statue of himself. He stood there like a statue and then started to move when people tried to have their pictures taken with him.

COMPANIES GET IN THE ACT

More and more, companies have gotten into the April Fools spirit with false announcements or unlikely events. The goal is to get good publicity for themselves and to make people smile. Companies that launch April Fools on the world usually send out a press announcement at noon making clear it was a joke.

April
Fools'
Day

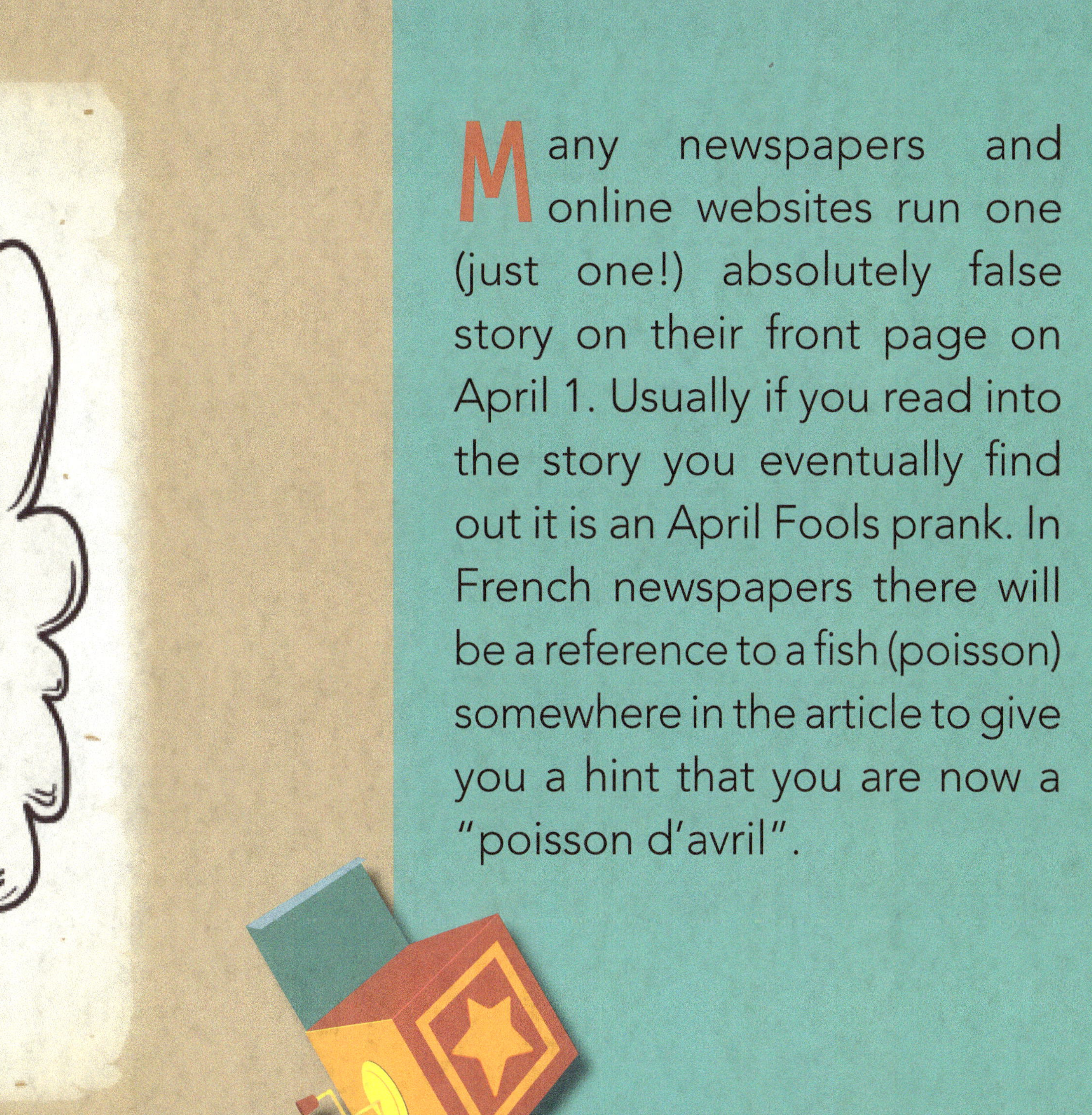

Many newspapers and online websites run one (just one!) absolutely false story on their front page on April 1. Usually if you read into the story you eventually find out it is an April Fools prank. In French newspapers there will be a reference to a fish (poisson) somewhere in the article to give you a hint that you are now a "poisson d'avril".

One of the most famous pranks was on April 1, 1957. The BBC ran a video story about Swiss farmers getting a better crop from their spaghetti trees, now that they had figured out how to combat the dreaded spaghetti weevil. So many viewers called or wrote in asking where they could get their own spaghetti trees that the network had to confess it was a joke.

In 1980 a Boston television station ran a made-up story about a volcanic explosion at Great Blue Hill, a small hill near Boston. This started a panic, with people fleeing their homes. The producer of the show had to be fired for not considering that people might take the story seriously and react to it.

anada has one-dollar (loonie) and two-dollar (toonie) coins. In 2008 on April 1, CBC Radio announced that the government planned to release a three-dollar coin (the "threenie") and to stop using the five-dollar bill.

3
DOLLARS
1854

In 2009 on April 1, a company announced the first launch of its helicopter hotel. The joke was to draw attention to the company's hotel-finding service.

One year on April 1, Google announced in the Netherlands that it would offer self-driving bicycles.

The town of Ely, Minnesota, which has a tradition of "official" April Fools gags, announced one year they had obtained a supply of canoe paddles with built-in propellers and motors that residents could rent.

AN UNLUCKY DAY?

Some people believe that April 1 is an unlucky day in itself, and not just because people may be playing tricks on you. Businesses avoid planning big events or announcements for April 1, partly because it might be bad luck and partly because they think people will think the announcement is a joke. Google made a big announcement about its email system on April 1 one year, and many people refused to believe it for days.

APRIL
1

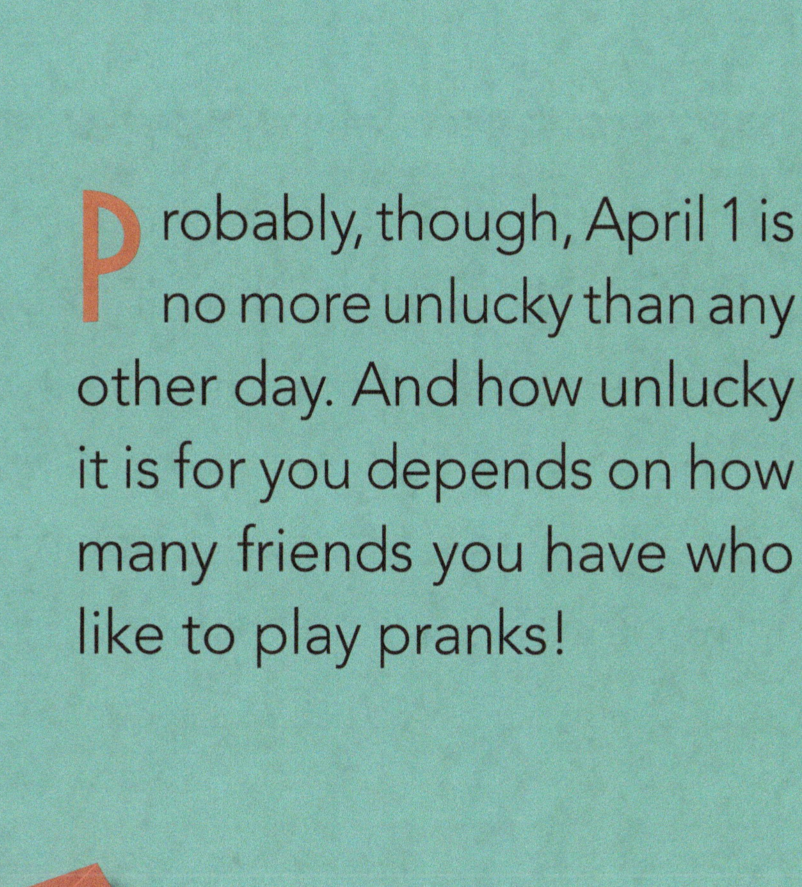

Probably, though, April 1 is no more unlucky than any other day. And how unlucky it is for you depends on how many friends you have who like to play pranks!

SOME RULES FOR APRIL FOOLS

In England, Canada, the United States, and other countries that got their traditions from England, you have to play your April-Fools joke before noon. If you try to trick someone after the middle of the day, it is you who becomes the April Fool.

APRIL
1
KICK
ME!

April
Fools
day

The next important thing is that the prank has to involve fooling people. You can't just pop a balloon at them to surprise them. A prank that involves fooling could be to glue a nice, bright coin to the sidewalk so people can see and touch it, but can't pick it up. If you have boxes of cold cereal in your kitchen, switch the inner bags of two boxes, so the contents don't match the box.

If you plan to set up an April-Fools prank, remember that the point is to fool someone else, not to hurt them or make them sad. You want to be a great prankster, not a bully, and you certainly don't want to cause damage to a person or their property.

April's Fool

AH AH

When the prank happens, even the April Fool him or herself should end up laughing. Save the scary pranks for Halloween.

Remember, also, that not all people understand or appreciate the April Fools tradition. If people are new to your country, you might scare them or make them feel hated if something strange and unusual happens to them. It is not enough to have a funny idea: you have to have the right audience for your joke, too.

Finally, if your prank involves a mess, be ready to help clean it up. You don't just get to laugh and walk away, because then what you have done is not a joke at all.

LEARN MORE ABOUT HOLIDAYS

Holidays are more fun when you understand what they celebrate, and how they developed. Look for more Baby Professor books where you can learn about other holidays.

Visit

BABY PROFESSOR
EDUCATION KIDS

www.BabyProfessorBooks.com
to download Free Baby Professor eBooks and view
our catalog of new and exciting Children's Books